T0131990

150 Puzzles and Solutions to Make You Smarter

The KENKEN® Method

Puzzles for Beginners

KenKen: Math & Logic Puzzles That Will Make You Smarter!
Series editor: Robert Fuhrer (*KenKen Puzzle LLC, USA*)

ISSN: 2529-8003

KenKen: Math & Logic Puzzles That Will Make You Smarter! Vol. 1

150
Puzzles and
Solutions to
Make You
Smarter

The KENKEN® Method
Puzzles for Beginners

Created by
Tetsuya Miyamoto

Edited collection by

Robert Fuhrer
Founder, KenKen Puzzle Company

 **World Scientific**

NEW JERSEY · LONDON · SINGAPORE · BEIJING · SHANGHAI · HONG KONG · TAIPEI · CHENNAI · TOKYO

Published by

World Scientific Publishing Co. Pte. Ltd.
5 Toh Tuck Link, Singapore 596224
USA office: 27 Warren Street, Suite 401-402, Hackensack, NJ 07601
UK office: 57 Shelton Street, Covent Garden, London WC2H 9HE

British Library Cataloguing-in-Publication Data
A catalogue record for this book is available from the British Library.

KenKen: Math & Logic Puzzles That Will Make You Smarter! — Vol. 1
The KENKEN Method — Puzzles for Beginners
150 Puzzles and Solutions to Make You Smarter

ISBN 978-981-3232-55-6 (pbk)

For any available supplementary material, please visit
http://www.worldscientific.com/worldscibooks/10.1142/10778#t=suppl

Printed in Singapore

CONTENTS

INTRODUCTION

Welcome to KenKen! You may want to cancel your appointments, lock the doors, pull down the shades, and turn off your phone. Because you'll soon discover that KenKen is very addictive! It's a grid-based numerical puzzle that uses the basic math operations — addition, subtraction, multiplication, and division. Don't worry, you definitely don't need to be a math wiz to enjoy these puzzles! Just as important are your logic and problem-solving skills. You can even think of KenKen like a game of pool or chess: The more you think ahead to your upcoming moves and consider all the possible outcomes, the better you'll get!

KenKen was developed in 2004 by…no, not two guys named Ken… Japanese teacher and puzzlemaster Tetsuya Miyamoto. "Ken" translates to "wisdom" in Japanese, so KenKen means "wisdom squared." True to its name, the puzzle can actually make you smarter the more you play.

KenKen quickly became a sensation in Japan. And since arriving in Europe and the United States in 2008, the puzzle has gained a worldwide devoted following of all ages, backgrounds, and skill levels.

There's a good chance you can find KenKen in your local newspaper — the puzzle is printed in over 150 of them, including The New York Times (U.S.), The Times (U.K.), Der Spiegel Online (Germany), El Pais (Spain), the Globe and Mail (Canada), and many more. Over 50 million KenKen puzzles are played online annually. An international tournament is hosted in the U.S. every year, attracting adults and students alike, many from as far away as Asia and the Middle East. And over 30,000 teachers worldwide use KenKen in their classrooms to educate their students…hand to "make math fun!"

You are the latest to join the KenKen revolution! We're excited for you to try it out, and we bet you'll be excited too.

Robert Fuhrer,
Founder, KenKen Puzzle LLC

HOW TO USE THIS BOOK

Whether you're new to KenKen or an old pro, there's a KenKen puzzle for you!

In KenKen, there are grid sizes from 3×3 to 9×9. In general, the larger the square count, the harder the puzzle gets. In other words, a 4×4 grid size KenKen is usually more difficult than a 3×3 grid size KenKen puzzle; a 5×5 grid size KenKen is generally harder than 4×4, and so on (although a Difficult 4×4 or 5×5 puzzle can often be harder than an Easy puzzle one grid size larger).

In this book, the puzzles start at the 3×3 grid size, moving up to 6×6.

First time KenKen players are encouraged to get familiar with how to solve KenKen puzzles by working on the 3×3 puzzles. Once you've gained some experience and grow in confidence, continue to challenge yourselves up to the 6×6 grid size puzzles so that you can experience the full depth and complexity of KenKen — and stimulate your brain at the same time!

KenKen puzzles are offered from the Easy to Medium levels within each grid size.

As noted above, grid size is NOT the only factor that determines the difficulty level of KenKen. Within each grid size from 4×4 to 9×9, KenKen has a variety of difficulty levels, ranging from Easiest, Easy, and Medium to Hard and Expert (3×3 puzzles are always Easy). To solve KenKen puzzles, you will need to use your logic, reasoning and math skills. For more difficult puzzles, you'll have to employ more advanced logic to solve the puzzles.

This book contains puzzles categorized as Easiest, Easy and Medium for the 4×4 and 5×5 grid sizes, and Easiest and Easy for the 6×6 grid size, allowing you to hone your skills by solving a variety of difficulty levels.

Fill in the solving time.

There is a box next to each KenKen puzzle where you can input your solving time. Write down the time it takes you to complete each puzzle. As you continue to solve KenKen puzzles, you will be able to increase your speed while maintaining accuracy. Use the times to mark your progress!

Solutions can be found in the back of the book.

The solutions can be found in the back of the book…but no cheating! Try solving each puzzle before checking your work.

Enjoy the world of KenKen!

The inventor of KenKen, Tetsuya Miyamoto, always says "The rival is not the person next to you. It's the YOU from yesterday. The more you challenge yourself, the more you will improve. Day by day, KenKen will help you grow!" To support Miyamoto-sensei's vision, we added a Solving Time section next to each puzzle so that you can track your progress and see how your skills improve. Good luck…and enjoy the wonders of KenKen!

THE RULES OF KENKEN

**Your goal is to fill in the whole grid
with numbers, making sure no number is
repeated in any row or column.**

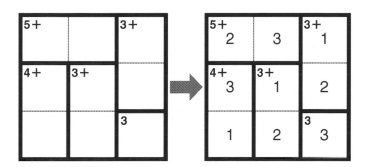

In a 3×3 puzzle, use the numbers 1–3.

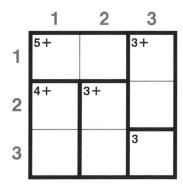

**In a 4×4 puzzle, use the numbers 1–4.
In a 5×5, use the numbers 1–5, and so on.**

5+		3+
4+	3+	
		3

The top left corner of each cage has a "target number" and math operation. The numbers you enter into a cage must combine (in any order) to produce the target number using the math operation noted (+, −, ×, or ÷)

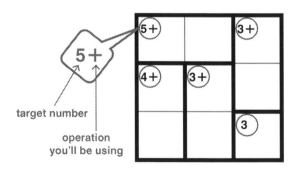

In this cage, the math operation to use is addition, and the numbers must add up to 5. Since the cage has 2 squares, the only possibilities are 2 and 3, in either order (2+3 or 3+2=5).

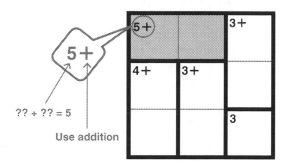

A cage with one square is a "Freebie"... just fill in the number you're given.

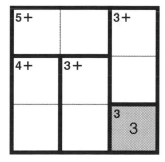

A number cannot be repeated within the same row or column.

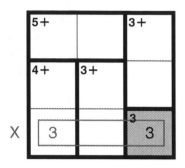

And that's it!

Solving a KenKen puzzle involves pure logic and mathematics.

No guesswork will ever be needed, and each puzzle has only one solution. So sharpen your pencil, sharpen your brain, and get started! In an instant, you'll know why Will Shortz, NPR Puzzle Master and The New York Times Puzzle editor calls KenKen "The most addictive puzzle since Sudoku!"

STEP-BY-STEP TUTORIAL FOR BEGINNERS

1. Let's start with a 3×3 KenKen grid. It will only contain the numbers 1, 2 and 3. These numbers must appear in every row and column, and no number can be repeated in any row or column.

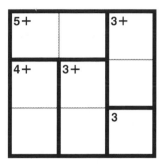

2. The first thing you'll want to do is look for any "freebie" squares. A "freebie" is an individual square, bordered with bold lines, with just a number (and no math operation) in the upper left corner. Just write that number in the square (like the 3 below) and voila, you've got a freebie!

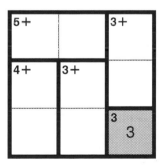

3. After freebies, we'll look for other cages which contain only 2 squares. Let's try the 4+ cage on the left side of the grid. The 4+ tells us we need to fill in those squares with two numbers that add up to 4. It's a 3×3 grid, so we can only use the numbers 1, 2 and 3. So it has to be either 1+3 or 2+2.

But…it can't be 2+2 because no number can be repeated in a row or column, and that would be two 2s in the left column. So it MUST be 1+3.

But wait, in which square does the 1 go and where does the 3 go? The 3 can't go in the bottom square because that row already has a 3 in it. So the 3 goes in the top square and the 1 goes in the bottom. Cage complete!

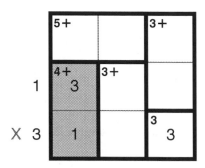

4. Remember, each row and column in this grid must have a 1, 2 and 3 in it. Our bottom row already has a 1 and 3, so a 2 must go in the row's middle square. With the same logic, we can complete the left column. Two more cages done!

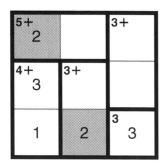

5. Now let's look at the 5+ cage in the top row. We've already filled in a 2 in one of its squares. So a 3 must go in the other square, because 2+3=5.

In the middle column, we already have a 3 and a 2, so a 1 must go in that middle square. That also satisfies the 3+ cage in the middle column.

5+ 2	3	3+
4+ 3	3+ 1	
1	2	3 3

6. Using our 1/2/3 in a row logic, we can put a 1 in the top right square and a 2 in the square below it. That also fulfills the 3+ cage in the right column. Great grid! Looks like you're ready for some real KenKens!

5+ 2	3	3+ 1
4+ 3	3+ 1	2
1	2	3 3

Your Hosts... The Two Kens

- *Hi, I'm Ken.*

- *And I'm Ken.*

- *We didn't invent KenKen.*

- *We're just two guys named Ken who like to play KenKen.*

- *We're going to teach you some tips, tricks, and secrets to get you up to speed on the world's fastest growing brain training math and logic puzzle.*

- *Pretty soon, you'll be a KenKen expert. Just like my buddy Ken.*

- *And my good friend Ken.*

- *Let's get started!*

3×3 PUZZLES

Addition

Let's start with the easiest types of KenKens…3×3 addition only puzzles…to grasp the basic rules. The goal is to fill each square using only the numbers 1, 2 and 3 without repeating a number in any row or column.

Remember, a "freebie" is always a great place to start. In Puzzle 1, fill in the "3" in the bottom left corner first, and you're on your way!

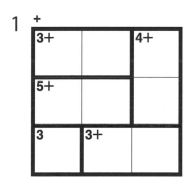

1

SOLVING TIME

2 +

```
3    5+   3+

3+

     4+
```

Now, let's try some puzzles with L-shaped cages that have 3 squares. You can repeat the same number in this type of cage *if* the squares you put the repeating numbers in are NOT in the same row or column.

3 +

```
3+        7+

6+

          2
```

4 +

5+	5+	
	6+	
		2

SOLVING TIME

[ ]

Here are some puzzles without any freebies. For these, the key is to identify cages that have only one possible combination of numbers. In some cases, you will be using your deductive skills. For example, if you already have a 1 and 2 in a row or column, the remaining square MUST be a 3, since numbers can't repeat.

Take a few seconds to look over the full puzzle before you begin. It's a great way to quickly pick out some of the easier-to-solve cages.

SOLVING TIME

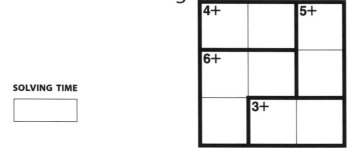

Great job!

You have done your first five 3×3 KenKens!

Addition & Subtraction

Let's now add subtraction to our puzzles. For a subtraction cage, you can arrange the numbers *in any order*. If the cage says 2−, the difference in the cage must be 2…but should it be [3, 1] or [1, 3]?

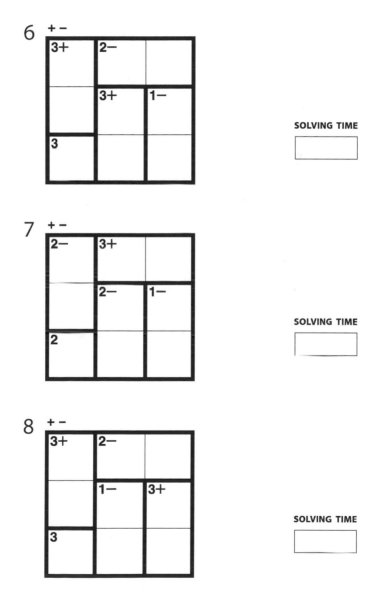

6 + −

3+	2−	
	3+	1−
3		

SOLVING TIME

7 + −

2−	3+	
	2−	1−
2		

SOLVING TIME

8 + −

3+	2−	
	1−	3+
3		

SOLVING TIME

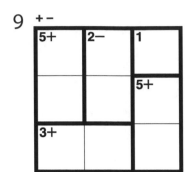

9 + −

5+	2−	1
		5+
3+		

Here's a no-freebie addition and subtraction puzzle. Remember, you can repeat a number if it is not in the same column or row within an L-shaped cage.

10 + −

3+		5+
6+		
	2−	

Great job!

You have conquered KenKen with addition AND subtraction!

As with baking, ping pong, and playing the bassoon, when it comes to KenKen, practice makes perfect. The more puzzles you do, the faster your brain will process the next one! Keep going...you'll see exactly what we mean.

All Four Operations

Let's try puzzles that use Addition, Subtraction, Multiplication and Division. Just like Subtraction, you can put numbers in any order for a division cage. (For example, if the target number is 2÷, you can put either [2, 1] or [1, 2].) The following puzzles let you start with a freebie. Remember to do those first!

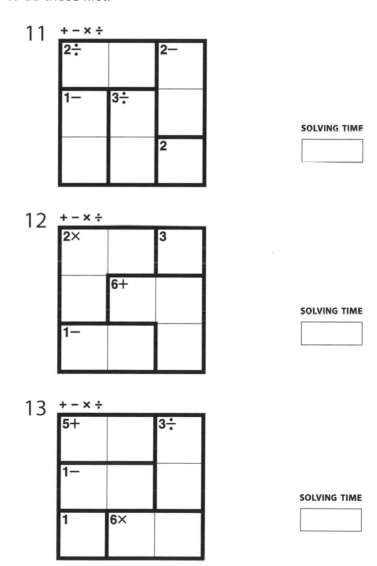

11   + − × ÷

2÷		2−
1−	3÷	
		2

SOLVING TIME

12   + − × ÷

2×		3
	6+	
1−		

SOLVING TIME

13   + − × ÷

5+		3÷
1−		
1	6×	

SOLVING TIME

14 **+ − × ÷**

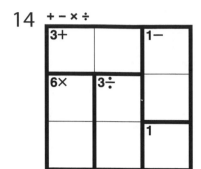

Now, let's try a 3×3 All Operations KenKen without any freebies! The key is always to find a cage that has only one combination of numbers. That should point you in the right direction…

15 **+ − × ÷**

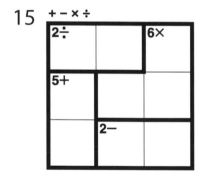

Great job!

You have now conquered the art of solving 3×3 KenKens!

It's time to move on to 4×4 puzzles.

4×4 puzzles will take a bit more thought and concentration, and a bit more time, but the techniques you'll use are the same. In fact, the same thought processes can be used for all KenKen puzzles, including the most challenging 9×9 Expert puzzles!

4×4 PUZZLES (Easiest Level)

Addition

Let's move on to 4×4 addition-only puzzles. Remember, in these larger 4×4 grids, you will use the numbers 1, 2, 3 and 4, as long as you only use each number once in each row and column.

16 +

3+	2	7+	
	7+		3+
7+	5+		
	3+		3

SOLVING TIME

17 +

5+		4	4+
6+	5+	4+	
			2
4+		6+	

SOLVING TIME

9

18 +

1	5+	5+	6+
7+			
	3+		7+
6+			

SOLVING TIME

19 +

3+	5+		7+
	6+	7+	
			2
7+		3+	

SOLVING TIME

Let's try a 4×4 addition puzzle without any freebies!

20 **+**

6+	3+		4+
	4+	6+	
4+			6+
	7+		

SOLVING TIME

Sometimes, addition-only puzzles are HARDER because there are more possible number combinations in each cage, especially in larger grid sizes. Appearances...they are deceiving!

Now you're getting the hang of it!

You have conquered 4×4 addition-only KenKen puzzles!

They're more challenging than 3×3s, and they help exercise your mind.

Addition & Subtraction

Now, let's add subtraction to some of the cages. The potential number combinations increase when the grid size gets larger, but the basic rules of KenKen remain the same.

Remember, numbers can be arranged in any order within a cage when using subtraction.

21 + −

2−	2	4+	
	7+	5+	3−
2−			
	3−		2

SOLVING TIME

22 + −

7+		2	3−
3+		4+	
1−	3−		3
		6+	

SOLVING TIME

23 + −

6+		2−	
3−	3	7+	3+
	6+		
		2−	

24 + −

1−	3−		1−
	7+		
3−	3+		10+
	2		

Here's another…with NO FREEBIES!

25 + −

1−	1−		7+
	2−	3−	
7+			3+
	6+		

SOLVING TIME

Ken-gratulations!

**You have conquered 4×4 addition and subtraction
KenKen puzzles!**

All Four Operations

Let's try some 4×4 KenKens using all four math operations! Once you complete this set of puzzles, including the ones without freebies, you will be ready to move up to more challenging KenKens!

26 + − × ÷

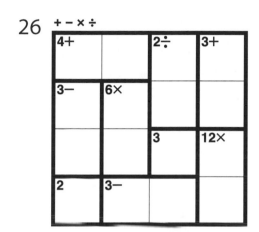

4+		2÷	3+
3−	6×		
		3	12×
2	3−		

SOLVING TIME

27 + − × ÷

3	2÷	3−	6×
3−			
	5+		1
2÷		7+	

SOLVING TIME

28

+ − × ÷

2÷		1	12×
2	2−		
4+		2−	2÷
7+			

29

+ − × ÷

3	3+		2÷
3−	4+		
	2	12×	
2−		2−	

30

+ − × ÷

2÷	7+		24×
	2÷	3−	
3			
1−		2÷	

31 + − × ÷

4+	2÷		8×
	7+	2−	
2÷			
	3+		3

SOLVING TIME

32 + − × ÷

2÷		1−	
36×		1	6+
3−		16×	

SOLVING TIME

33 + − × ÷

3−	7+		1−
	2−	2÷	
2			4×
6×			

SOLVING TIME

17

Here are a couple more 4×4 All Four Operations KenKens without any freebies. Don't worry...they'll still be pretty easy for now. Harder puzzles will appear later in the book.

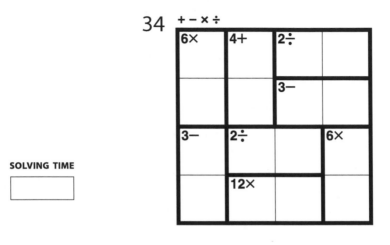

34 + − × ÷

6×	4+	2÷	
		3−	
3−	2÷		6×
	12×		

SOLVING TIME

35 + − × ÷

2÷	6×		3−
	1−		
5+		6×	
7+		2÷	

SOLVING TIME

4×4 PUZZLES (Easy Level)

Addition

You have now mastered the easiest level of 4×4 puzzles, and are able to work with all types of math operations. Now let's try some that are a bit harder.

36 +

3+		7+	
9+	7+		6+
	3+		
	5+		

SOLVING TIME

37 +

6+			9+
7+	5+		
	3+		
6+		4+	

SOLVING TIME

When you see an I-shaped cage of 3 squares that uses addition in a 4×4 puzzle, use deductive logic to figure out the 4th square in that row or column. The sum of the entire row or column (and ANY row or column in a 4×4) MUST be 10 (1+2+3+4=10). If the target number in a 3-square I-shaped cage is [6+], the one square left in that row or column must be a 4 (since 10−6=4).

38 +

6+	3+		6+
	5+	7+	
			6+
7+			

SOLVING TIME

[   ]

39 +

5+		8+	
9+		5+	
			4+
4	5+		

SOLVING TIME

[   ]

40 +

5+		8+	
7+	2		3+
	4+	9+	
2			

SOLVING TIME

Sometimes, you might know which numbers have to go in a cage, but not know the order (2+3 or 3+2?). Mark your options down in pencil and come back to them when you've filled in more of the numbers around them.

Great Job!

You just conquered 4×4 addition only Easy level KenKens!

Addition & Subtraction

41 + −

7+		2−	3+
2−	1−		
		3	1−
2	3−		

SOLVING TIME

42 + −

1−	3−	7+	
		3+	1
7+			2−
6+			

SOLVING TIME

22

43 + −

6+			6+
3	3−		
3−		6+	
2−		3	

SOLVING TIME

44 + −

8+	3−		3
		7+	3+
2−	1		
	9+		

SOLVING TIME

45 +−

2−		7+	3+
5+	5+		
		8+	
3	3+		

SOLVING TIME

[ ]

Great job!

You just conquered your first easy level 4×4 Addition and Subtraction KenKens! But this is no time to stop. In the next section, you'll find some manageable All Operations 4×4 puzzles, followed by more challenging puzzles with higher difficulty levels and grid sizes.

All Four Operations

46   + − × ÷

6×	3−		3
	2−		3+
1−		1	
2÷		1−	

SOLVING TIME

47   + − × ÷

2÷		12×	
4+		2	
1−	4+	2÷	
			3

SOLVING TIME

25

48 +−×÷

3−		18×	2
1	8+		
1−			5+
	2÷		

SOLVING TIME

49 +−×÷

6×		4+	2−
3−			
8×		1−	
3		2÷	

SOLVING TIME

50 +−×÷

7+	6×	2÷	
			3−
1−	2−	3	
		4+	

SOLVING TIME

51

+ − × ÷

9+		2÷	1
8×			7+
	9×		
		2−	

SOLVING TIME

52

+ − × ÷

2÷		2−	2÷
7+			
3−	6×	1−	
		2÷	

SOLVING TIME

53

+ − × ÷

1−	2÷		3−
	7+	6×	
2÷			6×
	3−		

SOLVING TIME

27

54

+ − × ÷

7+	6×		2÷
	3−		
2÷	1−	5+	
		6×	

55

+ − × ÷

3+		12×	
7+	2÷		
	6×	6×	
		3−	

Ken-gratulations!

You're clearly becoming a skilled KenKen solver, but we think you can do more. Are you ready to think a bit harder?

4×4 PUZZLES (Medium Level)

Addition

KenKen puzzles can range from very easy to terrifyingly tough within each grid size. If you've gotten this far, you clearly understand the basics and can do 4×4 puzzles in the "easy" range. You're now ready for a greater challenge. Try these slightly more difficult puzzles, categorized in the Medium difficulty range.

56 +

5+	7+		8+
	3+		
9+	2	6+	

SOLVING TIME

57 +

3+		9+	5+
9+			
		6+	
1	7+		

SOLVING TIME

29

58 +

9+		4+	5+
2			
7+	6+		7+

SOLVING TIME

59 +

9+	1	7+	
		7+	
8+			5+
3			

SOLVING TIME

60 +

8+	3+		6+
		12+	
5+	6+		

SOLVING TIME

One thing we forgot to tell you...there's no guessing necessary in KenKen, so don't bother guessing! Narrow down your options methodically until there's only one possible answer for each square. You can use this strategy for 4×4 puzzles, 5×5 puzzles, and even 9×9 puzzles (when you're brave enough to tackle them).

Ken-gratulations!

We knew you could solve challenging puzzles.

Here are some more...

Addition & Subtraction

61 + −

2	7+		1−
5+	1−	1	
		1−	
2−		6+	

SOLVING TIME

62 + −

1−		1−	
6+	3−		2−
	9+		
3		3+	

SOLVING TIME

63 + −

2−		2−	
3−		1−	
2−	1−	9+	
			2

SOLVING TIME

64 + −

8+	**1−**		**3−**
		4	
3−	**2**	**6+**	
	1−		

SOLVING TIME

KenKen puzzles come in all different configurations, and can have cages with many squares in many different shapes. Here's a KenKen with a cage that consists of 4 squares combined to form one larger square (see bottom left). Remember, you can repeat a number as long as it doesn't repeat in the same row or column. In this type of cage, the numbers diagonal to each other can repeat.

65 + −

7+	**2−**		**2−**
		4+	
9+			**2−**
		4	

SOLVING TIME

Great!

4×4 Medium Level KenKens with subtraction are clearly no problem for you! Coming up...

All Four Operations!

33

All Four Operations

66 +−×÷

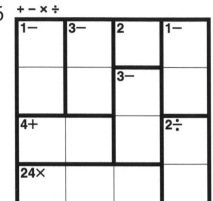

SOLVING TIME

67 +−×÷

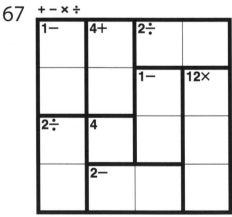

SOLVING TIME

68

+ − × ÷

8+	1	6×	
		1−	2÷
1−	2÷		
		3−	

SOLVING TIME

69

+ − × ÷

1−		12×	
7+	2÷	2−	
			1
3−		1−	

SOLVING TIME

70

+ − × ÷

1−	2−	8×	2
2÷	1−		7+
	3−		

SOLVING TIME

71

+ − × ÷

2÷	4	6×	
	1−	5+	
2−			7+
	3+		

SOLVING TIME

72

+ − × ÷

8×	2÷		7+
1−	2−	16×	
			2

SOLVING TIME

73

+ − × ÷

4×		1−	5+
7+			
	10+	2÷	
			3

SOLVING TIME

74

+ − × ÷

2÷		3−	6×
5+	3−		
		1−	
1−		2÷	

SOLVING TIME

75

+ − × ÷

2÷		4+	
7+	1−		2÷
	5+		
2÷		12×	

SOLVING TIME

Ready for a new challenge?

Let's move on to 5×5 KenKens! These will have different number combinations, and will require a bit more concentration.

5×5 PUZZLES (Easiest Level)

Addition

Some 5×5s can be quite manageable, while others can test even the best solvers. Let's start with some very easy puzzles to get warmed up. When doing 5×5 puzzles, you will use the numbers 1, 2, 3, 4 and 5 to fill the puzzle.

76 +

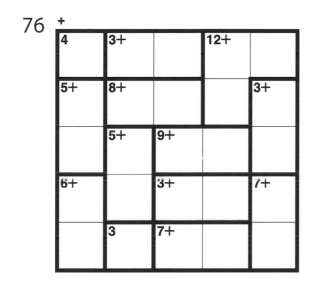

SOLVING TIME

77 +

8+		1	9+	6+
3+		5+		
9+			4+	
5+	9+		3+	8+
	5+			

78 +

6+	7+		7+	
		5+	9+	3+
9+	4+			
		5	3+	8+
2	7+			

SOLVING TIME

79 +

3+	6+		4+	9+
	4+	8+		
12+			7+	3+
	9+			
	3+		7+	

SOLVING TIME

80 +

3+	7+		6+	
	10+			9+
7+		3+		
8+	9+		3+	
	3+		7+	

SOLVING TIME

You're off to a good start...

You just conquered your first "easiest level" 5×5 KenKens!

41

Addition & Subtraction

Now, let's add subtraction to some 5×5 puzzles.

As you try solving these puzzles, fill in possible answers in pencil (most people write small numbers at the bottom of the squares or on the lines) and erase them as you narrow down the possibilities.

81 + −

7+		5+	4−	
4−			6+	
5+	9+	8+		
		4	4+	
3+		8+		4

SOLVING TIME

82 + −

3+	5+		9+	5
	4+			3−
8+	9+	2−		
		4−	4+	5+
6+				

SOLVING TIME

83 + −

7+	1	8+	9+	
			3+	7+
4	4−			
4−	7+		3−	
	6+		4+	

SOLVING TIME

84 + −

10+		3+	9+	2
4−				4+
	9+		3+	
6+		3		1−
3+		8+		

SOLVING TIME

43

85 + −

6+	5+		9+	6+
	4−			
	13+	3+	8+	
			7+	4+
8+				

SOLVING TIME

Good work!

It's time to move on to our easiest 5×5 all four operations puzzles.

44

All Four Operations

Now let's try 5×5 puzzles using all four operations. You'll notice that as the grids get larger, the Target Numbers used in multiplication squares get bigger. That can be intimidating, but large numbers don't necessarily mean more possible solutions. Often, these cages have a limited number of correct combinations.

86 + − × ÷

12×		3+		5
3−	1−		6×	
	4−		4	
3+		5	45×	2÷
3−				

SOLVING TIME

87 + − × ÷

15×		3+	2÷	
7+	4−		9+	1
		3		1−
2÷	32×	4−		
			8+	

SOLVING TIME

45

+ − × ÷

2	4−		24×	
4−	36×		3+	
	2÷			6+
8+		15×		
		3−		4

SOLVING TIME

+ − × ÷

45×		2÷	3−	4−
2÷				
	2÷	3	13+	2−
4−				
	8×			3

SOLVING TIME

90 +−×÷

5+	2÷		18×	4−
	5			
6×	3+		20×	
	9+			1−
15×		3−		

SOLVING TIME

[ ]

91 +−×÷

15×		2÷		2÷
4−	1−		3+	
	32×	4−		3
			3	20×
2÷		2−		

SOLVING TIME

[ ]

92

+ − × ÷

10×	4−		36×	
	2÷		3+	
36×	20×			3+
		4−		
2÷		3	1−	

SOLVING TIME

93

+ − × ÷

2÷	4−	60×		
		3+	4+	2÷
15×	1−			
		48×	4−	
1			3−	

SOLVING TIME

48

94

+ − × ÷

4+		9+		2÷
6×		4−	48×	
20×	2			
	7+		2÷	2−
	12×			

SOLVING TIME

95

+ − × ÷

6×		2÷	9+	4−
	45×			
20×			3+	4
	3−			18×
	3−			

SOLVING TIME

Ken-gratulations!

Now that you can solve our easier 5×5s, you're ready to move on to a more challenging level.

5×5 PUZZLES (Easy Level)

Addition

Here are some addition-only 5×5 puzzles that are a bit more challenging. See how long they take you to complete.

Sometimes, addition-only puzzles are more difficult than puzzles with all four operations because they have more possible combinations to solve for the Target Number. Make sure you consider all possible combinations before you settle on your answer.

96 +

9+		2	6+	
6+	9+		3	
	3+	9+		
5+		9+		10+
	4+			

SOLVING TIME

51

97 +

6+	7+		3	5+
	9+			
9+		6+		9+
	8+	3+		
		10+		

SOLVING TIME

98 +

15+		4	6+	5+
3+				
		9+		10+
7+		3+		
5+		8+		

SOLVING TIME

99 +

3+		9+		9+
8+	10+	3+		
			9+	
4+		5+		6+
9+				

SOLVING TIME

 Remember, you can use the same number more than once in an "L-shaped" cage, provided the identical numerals are in different rows or columns.

100 +

3+	9+		5+	
	7+	10+		3+
8+			6+	
	7+	8+		9+

SOLVING TIME

Good work!

It's time to add subtraction to our puzzles...

Addition & Subtraction

101 + −

3+		3	4−	1−
5+	9+	3+		
			1−	
1−	3	6+		6+
	4−			

SOLVING TIME

102 + −

10+			1	5+
3+	7+	9+		
		1−		10+
9+		3+		
6+		7+		

SOLVING TIME

103

+ -

4−	7+	6+		9+
			6+	
2−		17+		
1−	4−			
		3−		2

SOLVING TIME

104

+ -

9+		2−	4+	
3+	2−		12+	
				3
8+	3+		15+	
	2−			

SOLVING TIME

105 + −

2−	9+			5
	9+			3+
8+		5+		
5+		7+	4−	1−
3−				

SOLVING TIME

Excellent!

Let's move on to some puzzles using all four operations.

All Four Operations

106   + − × ÷

12×	4−	2÷		3+
		7+	6+	
5+				1−
4−	30×			
	8×			3

SOLVING TIME

107   + − × ÷

2÷		1−	3−	5
75×				3−
1−		2÷		
	2÷	8+		1−
1		9+		

SOLVING TIME

57

108 + − × ÷

15×	1−	3	2−	
		2÷	8+	
	5		9+	6×
2−	4+			
	9+			

109 + − × ÷

9+	24×	9+		
			2÷	
6×	5+	3	1−	
		2÷		5
4−		24×		

110

+ − × ÷

3−		2	15×	
18×		10+		
3+		15×	2÷	1−
	1−			
5			2÷	

SOLVING TIME

111

+ − × ÷

2÷		60×	2÷	3
4−				7+
	4−	1−		
6×			9+	
	4	9+		

SOLVING TIME

59

112 + − × ÷

6+		**9+**	**9+**	**4+**
4	**3+**			
24×			**4+**	**3−**
		4−		
2−			**2÷**	

113 + − × ÷

75×	**3**	**3−**	**8+**	
				9+
2÷	**2÷**			
	1−		**9+**	
3+		**9+**		

114 +−×÷

75×		3+		8×
	1−	9+		
1			1−	
2÷	2÷		9+	8+
	2−			

SOLVING TIME

115 +−×÷

16×		5	2−	
	12×		6+	
4−		2÷		24×
60×		8+		
		3+		

SOLVING TIME

Ken-gratulations! It looks like you're a KenKen master.

Going forward, you won't need our tips...the solving concepts remain the same, regardless of puzzle difficulty or grid size.

You're about to solve more difficult 5×5s (rated as "Medium"), and then some 6×6s.

Good luck!

5×5 PUZZLES (Medium Level)

Addition

116 +

14+	11+	4	3+	
			9+	6+
	3+			
		10+	9+	
6+				

SOLVING TIME

117 +

9+		5+		3+
7+		9+		
8+		6+		15+
	10+			
			3	

SOLVING TIME

118 +

14+		3+		9+
9+				
	12+	6+	3+	
3+			12+	
				4

119 +

8+	5+		7+	8+
	12+	3+		
			6+	7+
		10+		
9+				

120 +

8+		9+	6+	
8+				8+
	6+			
11+			7+	
	3+		9+	

SOLVING TIME

Addition & Subtraction

121 + −

5+	7+		5	1−
	3+	13+		
1−				9+
	4−		2−	
10+				1

122 + −

7+	9+		8+	
	1−		2−	
11+	4−			4
	3+		1−	
		4	3−	

123 + −

3−		1−	3−	
7+			1−	
	7+	4−	1−	2
4				4−
1−		9+		

124 + −

3	9+		3+	
4−		11+		8+
1−		4−		
2−			13+	
3−				

125 + −

7+	3+		4−	5+
	1−			
9+		5	2−	
4−		8+		1−
	4+			

SOLVING TIME

All Four Operations

126   + − × ÷

2÷	1−		10×	
	10×	7+		9+
4−		2÷		6×
1−		5		

SOLVING TIME

127   + − × ÷

30×			9+	
4−	1−	2÷		
		4−	5+	
24×			40×	15×

SOLVING TIME

128 + − × ÷

2÷	1−	2−	4−	
			6×	
2−		3−	2÷	3−
8+				
7+			2−	

SOLVING TIME

129 + − × ÷

2÷		5	2−	
4+		40×		
3+	1−		40×	
	20×			1−
5		4+		

SOLVING TIME

130

+ − × ÷

120×		4−		2÷
		1−		
4−		2÷		12+
8×	2−		2	
		4+		

SOLVING TIME

131

+ − × ÷

10×		60×		
9+		2÷	1−	
	10+		50×	3−
1−				
	5+			

SOLVING TIME

71

132

+ - × ÷

15×		3+		1−
7+		6+		
	2−		2÷	
1−		2÷	75×	
2÷				

SOLVING TIME

133

+ - × ÷

12×		9+	2÷	
2−			2	6+
2÷	5+	1−	1−	
				1−
3−		2−		

SOLVING TIME

72

134

+ − × ÷

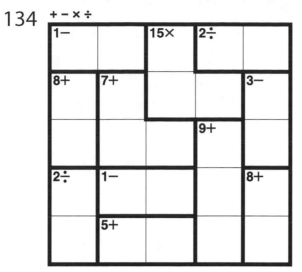

1−		15×	2÷	
8+	7+			3−
			9+	
2÷	1−			8+
	5+			

135

+ − × ÷

12×	2−	3+		40×
		5+	2−	
3+	1			
	1−		2÷	2−
5	1−			

6×6 PUZZLES (Easiest Level)

Addition

Ken-gratulations…you have completed the 5×5 challenges and are skilled enough to move on to the 6×6 grid size! Remember, for 6×6s, you use only the numbers 1, 2, 3, 4, 5 and 6. These puzzles are more challenging, but can also be more satisfying. Enjoy!

136 +

11+		5+		5+	
7+	5+		8+		5
	13+	4+		6+	7+
3+			11+		
	10+			5+	
6	3+		12+		

SOLVING TIME

75

137 +

8+	3+	11+			5+
		9+		11+	
7+		3+			8+
7+	11+		7+		
	10+		6+		8+
8+			4+		

SOLVING TIME

Addition & Subtraction

138 +−

2−		12+	2	4+	
2			5−		11+
4+	7+	7+		5	
		6	3+		2−
1−	5−		8+	10+	
	3+				3

SOLVING TIME

139 +−

5−		9+	16+		
9+	3−		3+		
		1−		5+	
9+		5+		5−	
5+		6+	16+		4+
7+			4		

SOLVING TIME

All Four Operations

140 + − × ÷

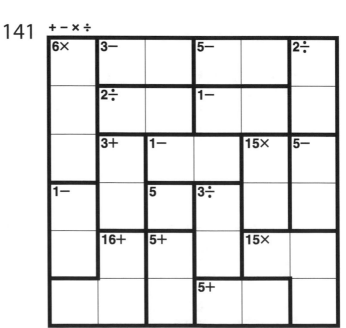

SOLVING TIME

141 + − × ÷

SOLVING TIME

142

+ − × ÷

5−	10+		10+	6×	
	3			9+	120×
2÷	4−	3÷			
			5−		
20×		3+		2÷	
8+		24×		2÷	

SOLVING TIME

143

+ − × ÷

24×		3÷	7+	50×	
3	20×				
3÷			11+		9+
		15×		72×	
3+					
2−		2÷		5−	

SOLVING TIME

144

+ − × ÷

10×	3÷		6	9+	
	1−	2÷		5−	2÷
3÷		9+			
	24×	3÷		6+	
10+		6+		3	8+
	5	3÷			

SOLVING TIME

145

+ − × ÷

16×	2÷		1−		5−
		15×			
6+	20×	2−		3+	6×
		4−	2−		
3÷				24×	
3−		3+		9+	

SOLVING TIME

6×6 PUZZLES (Easy Level)

All Four Operations

146 + − × ÷

2−		2	11+	6×	2÷
5−	6+	14+			
					2−
2−	3−		2÷		
	10+		7+	11+	
3−					1

SOLVING TIME

147 + − × ÷

10×		15+		5−	
5−	6+		9+		1−
			5+		
3	24×	1−	5−	10+	
2÷					6+
	3	9+			

SOLVING TIME

81

OK...one more tip. Now that you've moved on to bigger puzzles with more possible numbers, don't get freaked out by cages with big Target Numbers! They might look intimidating, but often they only have one solution. Once you solve these, you can be confident you can conquer any KenKen puzzle...all the way up to a 9×9. Enjoy!

148 + − × ÷

2−		3	30×		
3÷		11+		14+	5+
18×	10×				
		5+	3+	300×	
4−					
1−		2÷		2÷	

SOLVING TIME

149 + − × ÷

5−		12×	11+	3÷	2−
10×					
2−		2÷		10+	
2÷		3÷	60×		
2−	7+		7+		6+
		30×			

SOLVING TIME

82

150 + − × ÷

3÷	11+		2÷	3÷	
	5+			2−	
3−		15×	5−	40×	3÷
1−	2÷				
		1−			3−
6×			1−		

SOLVING TIME

Ken-gratulations...you've conquered them all.

You are now officially a KenKen Master!

SOLUTIONS

11

+ − × ÷

2÷		2−
1	**2**	**3**
1−	3÷	
2	**3**	**1**
		2
3	**1**	**2**

12

+ − × ÷

2×		3
2	**1**	**3**
	6+	
1	**3**	**2**
1−		
3	**2**	**1**

13

+ − × ÷

5+		3÷
3	**2**	**1**
1−		
2	**1**	**3**
1	6×	
1	**3**	**2**

14

+ − × ÷

3+		1−
1	**2**	**3**
6×	3÷	
3	**1**	**2**
		1
2	**3**	**1**

15

+ − × ÷

2÷		6×
1	**2**	**3**
5+		
3	**1**	**2**
	2−	
2	**3**	**1**

16

+

3+	2	7+	
1	**2**	**3**	**4**
	7+		3+
2	**3**	**4**	**1**
7+	5+		
3	**4**	**1**	**2**
	3+		3
4	**1**	**2**	**3**

17

+

5+		4	4+
3	**2**	**4**	**1**
6+	5+	4+	
2	**4**	**1**	**3**
			2
4	**1**	**3**	**2**
4+		6+	
1	**3**	**2**	**4**

18

+

1	5+	5+	6+
1	**3**	**4**	**2**
7+			
3	**2**	**1**	**4**
	3+		7+
4	**1**	**2**	**3**
6+			
2	**4**	**3**	**1**

19

+

3+	5+		7+
2	**4**	**1**	**3**
	6+	7+	
1	**2**	**3**	**4**
			2
3	**1**	**4**	**2**
7+		3+	
4	**3**	**2**	**1**

88

20 (+)

6+ 4	3+ 2	1	4+ 3
2	4+ 3	6+ 4	1
4+ 3	1	2	6+ 4
1	7+ 4	3	2

24 (+ −)

1− 3	3− 4	1	1− 2
2	7+ 3	4	1
3− 4	3+ 1	2	10+ 3
1	2 2	3	4

21 (+ −)

2− 4	2 2	4+ 1	3
2	7+ 4	5+ 3	3− 1
2− 1	3	2	4
3	3− 1	4	2 2

25 (+ −)

1− 1	1− 2	3	7+ 4
2	2− 1	3− 4	3
7+ 4	3	1	3+ 2
3	6+ 4	2	1

22 (+ −)

7+ 4	3	2 2	3− 1
3+ 1	2	4+ 3	4
1− 2	3− 4	1	3 3
3	1	6+ 4	2

26 (+ − × ÷)

4+ 3	1	2÷ 4	3+ 2
3− 4	6× 3	2	1
1	2	3 3	12× 4
2 2	3− 4	1	3

23 (+ −)

6+ 2	4	2− 1	3
3− 1	3 3	7+ 4	3+ 2
4	6+ 2	3	1
3	1	2− 2	4

27 (+ − × ÷)

3 3	2÷ 4	3− 1	6× 2
3− 1	2	4	3
4	5+ 3	2	1 1
2÷ 2	1	7+ 3	4

28

+ − × ÷

2÷ 4	2	**1** 1	**12×** 3
2 2	**2−** 1	3	4
4+ 1	3	**2−** 4	**2÷** 2
7+ 3	4	2	1

32

+ − × ÷

2÷ 2	1	**1−** 3	4
36× 3	4	**1** 1	**6+** 2
3− 4	3	**16×** 2	1
1	2	4	3

29

+ − × ÷

3 3	**3+** 1	2	**2÷** 4
3− 4	**4+** 3	1	2
1	**2** 2	**12×** 4	3
2− 2	4	**2−** 3	1

33

+ − × ÷

3− 1	**7+** 4	3	**1−** 2
4	**2−** 1	**2÷** 2	3
2 2	3	4	**4×** 1
6× 3	2	1	4

30

+ − × ÷

2÷ 1	**7+** 4	3	**24×** 2
2	**2÷** 1	**3−** 4	3
3 3	2	1	4
1− 4	3	**2÷** 2	1

34

+ − × ÷

6× 3	**4+** 1	**2÷** 2	4
2	3	**3−** 4	1
3− 4	**2÷** 2	1	**6×** 3
1	**12×** 4	3	2

31

+ − × ÷

4+ 3	**2÷** 2	4	**8×** 1
1	**7+** 4	**2−** 3	2
2÷ 2	3	1	4
4	**3+** 1	2	**3** 3

35

+ − × ÷

2÷ 1	**6×** 2	3	**3−** 4
2	**1−** 3	4	1
5+ 4	1	**6×** 2	3
7+ 3	4	**2÷** 1	2

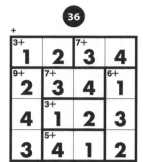

36 (+)

3+ 1	2	**7+** 3	4
9+ 2	**7+** 3	4	**6+** 1
4	**3+** 1	2	3
3	**5+** 4	1	2

37 (+)

6+ 1	3	2	**9+** 4
7+ 3	**5+** 1	4	2
4	**3+** 2	1	3
6+ 2	4	**4+** 3	1

38 (+)

6+ 3	**3+** 2	1	**6+** 4
1	**5+** 4	**7+** 3	2
2	1	4	**6+** 3
7+ 4	3	2	1

39 (+)

5+ 1	3	**8+** 2	4
9+ 3	1	**5+** 4	2
2	4	1	**4+** 3
4 4	**5+** 2	3	1

40 (+)

5+ 1	4	**8+** 2	3
7+ 4	**2** 2	3	**3+** 1
3	**4+** 1	**9+** 4	2
2 2	3	1	4

41 (+ −)

7+ 4	3	**2−** 2	**3+** 1
2− 3	**1−** 1	4	2
1	2	**3** 3	**1−** 4
2 2	**3−** 4	1	3

42 (+ −)

1− 2	**3−** 1	**7+** 4	3
3	4	**3+** 2	**1** 1
7+ 4	3	1	**2−** 2
6+ 1	2	3	4

43 (+ −)

6+ 2	3	1	**6+** 4
3 3	**3−** 1	4	2
3− 1	4	**6+** 2	3
2− 4	2	**3** 3	1

91

44
+ −

8+ 2	**3−** 4	1	**3** 3
4	2	**7+** 3	**3+** 1
2− 3	**1** 1	4	2
1	**9+** 3	2	4

45
+ −

2− 2	4	**7+** 3	**3+** 1
5+ 1	**5+** 3	4	2
4	2	**8+** 1	3
3 3	**3+** 1	2	4

46
+ − × ÷

6× 2	**3−** 1	4	**3** 3
3	**2−** 4	2	**3+** 1
1− 4	3	**1** 1	2
2÷ 1	2	**1−** 3	4

47
+ − × ÷

2÷ 2	4	**12×** 3	1
4+ 1	3	**2** 2	4
1− 3	**4+** 1	**2÷** 4	2
4	2	1	**3** 3

48
+ − × ÷

3− 4	1	**18×** 3	**2** 2
1 1	**8+** 4	2	3
1− 2	3	1	**5+** 4
3	**2÷** 2	4	1

49
+ − × ÷

6× 2	3	**4+** 1	**2−** 4
3− 4	1	3	2
8× 1	2	**1−** 4	3
3 3	4	**2÷** 2	1

50
+ − × ÷

7+ 3	**6×** 1	**2÷** 4	2
4	3	2	**3−** 1
1− 1	**2−** 2	**3** 3	4
2	4	**4+** 1	3

51
+ − × ÷

9+ 3	4	**2÷** 2	**1** 1
8× 4	2	1	**7+** 3
2	**9×** 1	3	4
1	3	**2−** 4	2

92

52

+ − × ÷

2÷ **2**	**1**	2− **3**	2÷ **4**
7+ **3**	**4**	**1**	**2**
3− **1**	6× **2**	1− **4**	**3**
4	**3**	2÷ **2**	**1**

56

+

5+ **2**	7+ **3**	**4**	8+ **1**
3	3+ **1**	**2**	**4**
9+ **4**	2 **2**	6+ **1**	**3**
1	**4**	**3**	**2**

53

+ − × ÷

1− **3**	2÷ **2**	**1**	3− **4**
4	7+ **3**	6× **2**	**1**
2÷ **1**	**4**	**3**	6× **2**
2	3− **1**	**4**	**3**

57

+

3+ **2**	**1**	9+ **3**	5+ **4**
9+ **3**	**4**	**2**	**1**
4	**2**	6+ **1**	**3**
1 **1**	7+ **3**	**4**	**2**

54

+ − × ÷

7+ **4**	6× **2**	**3**	2÷ **1**
3	3− **1**	**4**	**2**
2÷ **2**	1− **3**	5+ **1**	**4**
1	**4**	6× **2**	**3**

58

+

9+ **4**	**1**	4+ **3**	5+ **2**
2 **2**	**4**	**1**	**3**
7+ **3**	6+ **2**	**4**	7+ **1**
1	**3**	**2**	**4**

55

+ − × ÷

3+ **1**	**2**	12× **4**	**3**
7+ **3**	2÷ **4**	**2**	**1**
4	6× **1**	6× **3**	**2**
2	**3**	3− **1**	**4**

59

+

9+ **4**	1 **1**	7+ **2**	**3**
1	**4**	7+ **3**	**2**
8+ **2**	**3**	**4**	5+ **1**
3 **3**	**2**	**1**	**4**

60

+

8+ 4	**3+** 1	2	**6+** 3
1	3	**12+** 4	2
5+ 2	**6+** 4	3	1
3	2	1	4

64

+ −

8+ 3	**1−** 1	2	**3−** 4
2	3	**4** 4	1
3− 4	**2** 2	**6+** 1	3
1	**1−** 4	3	2

61

+ −

2 2	**7+** 4	3	**1−** 1
5+ 4	**1−** 3	**1** 1	2
1	2	**1−** 4	3
2− 3	1	**6+** 2	4

65

+ −

7+ 1	**2−** 4	2	**2−** 3
4	2	**4+** 3	1
9+ 2	3	1	**2−** 4
3	1	**4** 4	2

62

+ −

1− 1	2	**1−** 3	4
6+ 2	**3−** 1	4	**2−** 3
4	**9+** 3	2	1
3 3	4	**3+** 1	2

66

+ − × ÷

1− 3	**3−** 1	**2** 2	**1−** 4
2	4	**3−** 1	3
4+ 1	3	4	**2÷** 2
24× 4	2	3	1

63

+ −

2− 2	4	**2−** 3	1
3− 4	1	**1−** 2	3
2− 3	**1−** 2	**9+** 1	4
1	3	4	**2** 2

67

+ − × ÷

1− 4	**4+** 3	**2÷** 1	2
3	1	**1−** 2	**12×** 4
2÷ 2	**4** 4	3	1
1	**2−** 2	4	3

94

+ − × ÷

68

8+ 4	1	6× 2	3
1	3	1− 4	2÷ 2
1− 2	2÷ 4	3	1
3	2	3− 1	4

72

8× 1	2÷ 4	2	7+ 3
4	2	3	1
1− 2	2− 3	16× 1	4
3	1	4	2 2

69

1− 2	3	12× 1	4
7+ 4	2÷ 1	2− 2	3
3	2	4	1 1
3− 1	4	1− 3	2

73

4× 2	1	1− 3	5+ 4
7+ 3	2	4	1
4	10+ 3	2÷ 1	2
1	4	2	3 3

70

1− 3	2− 1	8× 4	2 2
4	3	2	1
2÷ 1	1− 2	3	7+ 4
2	3− 4	1	3

74

2÷ 1	2	3− 4	6× 3
5+ 3	3− 4	1	2
2	1	1− 3	4
1− 4	3	2÷ 2	1

71

2÷ 2	4 4	6× 3	1
4	1− 3	5+ 1	2
2− 1	2	4	7+ 3
3	3+ 1	2	4

75

2÷ 2	4	4+ 1	3
7+ 4	1− 3	2	2÷ 1
3	5+ 1	4	2
2÷ 1	2	12× 3	4

95

⁴4	³⁺2	1	¹²⁺3	5
⁵⁺2	⁸⁺5	3	4	³⁺1
3	⁵⁺1	⁹⁺4	5	2
⁶⁺5	4	³⁺2	1	⁷⁺3
1	³3	⁷⁺5	2	4

³⁺1	⁶⁺4	2	⁴⁺3	⁹⁺5
2	⁴⁺3	⁸⁺5	1	4
¹²⁺4	1	3	⁷⁺5	³⁺2
3	⁹⁺5	4	2	1
5	³⁺2	1	⁷⁺4	3

⁸⁺5	3	¹1	⁹⁺4	⁶⁺2
³⁺1	2	⁵⁺3	5	4
⁹⁺4	5	2	⁴⁺3	1
⁵⁺2	⁹⁺4	5	³⁺1	⁸⁺3
3	⁵⁺1	4	2	5

³⁺2	⁷⁺4	3	⁶⁺5	1
1	¹⁰⁺2	5	3	⁹⁺4
⁷⁺4	3	³⁺1	2	5
⁸⁺3	⁹⁺5	4	³⁺1	2
5	³⁺1	2	⁷⁺4	3

⁶⁺1	⁷⁺5	2	⁷⁺3	4
3	2	⁵⁺4	⁹⁺5	³⁺1
⁹⁺5	⁴⁺3	1	4	2
4	1	⁵5	³⁺2	⁸⁺3
²2	⁷⁺4	3	1	5

⁷⁺4	3	⁵⁺2	⁴⁻5	1
⁴⁻5	1	3	⁶⁺4	2
⁵⁺3	⁹⁺4	⁸⁺1	2	5
2	5	⁴4	⁴⁺1	3
³⁺1	2	⁸⁺5	3	⁴4

82 (+ -)

3+ **1**	5+ **3**	**2**	9+ **4**	5 **5**
2	4+ **1**	**3**	**5**	3- **4**
8+ **3**	9+ **5**	2- **4**	**2**	**1**
5	**4**	4- **1**	4+ **3**	5+ **2**
6+ **4**	**2**	**5**	**1**	**3**

85 (+ -)

6+ **1**	5+ **2**	**3**	9+ **5**	6+ **4**
3	4- **1**	**5**	**4**	**2**
2	13+ **4**	3+ **1**	8+ **3**	**5**
4	**5**	**2**	7+ **1**	4+ **3**
8+ **5**	**3**	**4**	**2**	**1**

83 (+ -)

7+ **2**	1 **1**	8+ **3**	9+ **4**	**5**
3	**2**	**5**	3+ **1**	7+ **4**
4 **4**	4- **5**	**1**	**2**	**3**
4- **1**	7+ **3**	**4**	3- **5**	**2**
5	6+ **4**	**2**	4+ **3**	**1**

86 (+ - × ÷)

12× **3**	**4**	3+ **2**	**1**	5 **5**
3- **5**	1- **3**	**4**	6× **2**	**1**
2	4- **5**	**1**	4 **4**	**3**
3+ **1**	**2**	5 **5**	45× **3**	2÷ **4**
3- **4**	**1**	**3**	**5**	**2**

84 (+ -)

10+ **3**	**4**	3+ **1**	9+ **5**	2 **2**
4- **5**	**3**	**2**	**4**	4+ **1**
1	9+ **5**	**4**	3+ **2**	**3**
6+ **4**	**2**	3 **3**	**1**	1- **5**
3+ **2**	**1**	8+ **5**	**3**	**4**

87 (+ - × ÷)

15× **5**	**3**	3+ **1**	2÷ **2**	**4**
7+ **3**	4- **5**	**2**	9+ **4**	1 **1**
4	**1**	3 **3**	**5**	1- **2**
2÷ **2**	32× **4**	4- **5**	**1**	**3**
1	**2**	**4**	8+ **3**	**5**

88

+ − × ÷

[2] 2	[4−] 5	1	[24×] 4	3
[4−] 5	[36×] 3	4	[3+] 1	2
1	[2÷] 4	3	2	[6+] 5
[8+] 4	2	[15×] 5	3	1
3	1	[3−] 2	5	[4] 4

89

+ − × ÷

[45×] 3	5	[2÷] 2	[3−] 4	[4−] 1
[2÷] 2	3	4	1	5
4	[2÷] 1	[3] 3	[13+] 5	[2−] 2
[4−] 1	2	5	3	4
5	[8×] 4	1	2	[3] 3

90

+ − × ÷

[5+] 1	[2÷] 2	4	[18×] 3	[4−] 5
4	[5] 5	3	2	1
[6×] 3	[3+] 1	2	[20×] 5	4
2	[9+] 4	5	1	[1−] 3
[15×] 5	3	[3−] 1	4	2

91

+ − × ÷

[15×] 3	5	[2÷] 2	4	[2÷] 1
[4−] 5	[1−] 3	4	[3+] 1	2
1	[32×] 4	[4−] 5	2	[3] 3
4	2	1	[3] 3	[20×] 5
[2÷] 2	1	[2−] 3	5	4

92

+ − × ÷

[10×] 2	[4−] 1	5	[36×] 3	4
5	[2÷] 4	2	[3+] 1	3
[36×] 3	[20×] 5	4	2	[3+] 1
4	3	[4−] 1	5	2
[2÷] 1	2	[3] 3	[1−] 4	5

93

+ − × ÷

[2÷] 2	[4−] 1	[60×] 5	4	3
4	5	[3+] 1	[4+] 3	[2÷] 2
[15×] 5	[1−] 3	2	1	4
3	2	[48×] 4	[4−] 5	1
[1] 1	4	3	[3−] 2	5

94

+ − × ÷

3 (4+)	**1**	**4** (9+)	**5**	**2** (2÷)
2 (6×)	**3**	**5** (4−)	**4** (48×)	**1**
5 (20×)	**2** (2)	**1**	**3**	**4**
4	**5** (7+)	**2**	**1** (2÷)	**3** (2−)
1	**4** (12×)	**3**	**2**	**5**

95

+ − × ÷

3 (6×)	**1**	**2** (2÷)	**4** (9+)	**5** (4−)
2	**3** (45×)	**4**	**5**	**1**
1 (20×)	**5**	**3**	**2** (3+)	**4** (4)
4	**2** (3−)	**5**	**1**	**3** (18×)
5	**4** (3−)	**1**	**3**	**2**

96

+

4 (9+)	**5**	**2** (2)	**1** (6+)	**3**
1 (6+)	**4** (9+)	**5**	**3** (3)	**2**
5	**1** (3+)	**3** (9+)	**2**	**4**
3 (5+)	**2**	**4** (9+)	**5**	**1** (10+)
2	**3** (4+)	**1**	**4**	**5**

97

+

4 (6+)	**2** (7+)	**5**	**3** (3)	**1** (5+)
2	**5** (9+)	**4**	**1**	**3**
3 (9+)	**1**	**2** (6+)	**4**	**5** (9+)
5	**3** (8+)	**1** (3+)	**2**	**4**
1	**4**	**3** (10+)	**5**	**2**

98

+

5 (15+)	**3**	**4** (4)	**2** (6+)	**1** (5+)
2 (3+)	**5**	**1**	**3**	**4**
1	**2**	**5** (9+)	**4**	**3** (10+)
3 (7+)	**4**	**2** (3+)	**1**	**5**
4 (5+)	**1**	**3**	**5** (8+)	**2**

99

+

2 (3+)	**1**	**5** (9+)	**4**	**3** (9+)
3 (8+)	**4** (10+)	**1** (3+)	**2**	**5**
5	**2**	**4**	**3** (9+)	**1**
1 (4+)	**3**	**2** (5+)	**5**	**4** (6+)
4 (9+)	**5**	**3**	**1**	**2**

100 +

3+ 1	9+ 5	4	5+ 2	3
2	7+ 3	10+ 5	4	3+ 1
8+ 3	4	1	6+ 5	2
5	7+ 2	8+ 3	1	9+ 4
4	1	2	3	5

101 + −

3+ 1	2	3 3	4− 5	1− 4
5+ 3	9+ 4	3+ 2	1	5
2	5	1	1− 4	3
1− 5	3 3	6+ 4	2	6+ 1
4	4− 1	5	3	2

102 + −

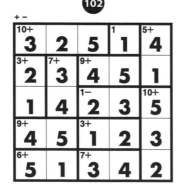

10+ 3	2	5	1 1	5+ 4
3+ 2	7+ 3	9+ 4	5	1
1	4	1− 2	3	10+ 5
9+ 4	5	3+ 1	2	3
6+ 5	1	7+ 3	4	2

103 + −

4− 5	7+ 3	6+ 2	1	9+ 4
1	4	3	6+ 2	5
2− 4	2	17+ 5	3	1
1− 2	4− 1	4	5	3
3	5	3− 1	4	2 2

104 + −

9+ 4	5	2− 3	4+ 1	2
3+ 2	2− 4	5	12+ 3	1
1	2	4	5	3 3
8+ 3	3+ 1	2	15+ 4	5
5	2− 3	1	2	4

105 + −

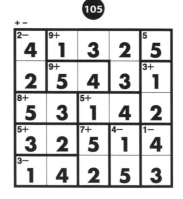

2− 4	9+ 1	3	2	5 5
2	9+ 5	4	3	3+ 1
8+ 5	3	5+ 1	4	2
5+ 3	2	7+ 5	4− 1	1− 4
3− 1	4	2	5	3

106

+ − × ÷

12× **3**	4− **5**	2÷ **2**	**4**	3+ **1**
4	**1**	7+ **3**	6+ **5**	**2**
5+ **2**	**3**	**4**	**1**	1− **5**
4− **1**	30× **2**	**5**	**3**	**4**
5	8× **4**	**1**	**2**	3 **3**

109

+ − × ÷

9+ **4**	24× **2**	9+ **5**	**3**	**1**
5	**3**	**4**	2÷ **1**	**2**
6× **2**	5+ **1**	3 **3**	1− **5**	**4**
3	**4**	2÷ **1**	**2**	5 **5**
4− **1**	**5**	24× **2**	**4**	**3**

107

+ − × ÷

2÷ **2**	**4**	1− **3**	**1**	5 **5**
75× **5**	**3**	**2**	**4**	3− **1**
1− **3**	**5**	2÷ **1**	**2**	**4**
4	2÷ **1**	8+ **5**	**3**	1− **2**
1 **1**	**2**	9+ **4**	**5**	**3**

110

+ − × ÷

3− **4**	**1**	2 **2**	15× **3**	**5**
18× **3**	**2**	10+ **4**	**5**	**1**
3+ **1**	**3**	15× **5**	2÷ **2**	1− **4**
2	1− **5**	**1**	**4**	**3**
5 **5**	**4**	**3**	2÷ **1**	**2**

108

+ − × ÷

15× **5**	1− **1**	3 **3**	2− **2**	**4**
1	**2**	2÷ **4**	8+ **3**	**5**
3	5 **5**	**2**	9+ **4**	6× **1**
2− **4**	4+ **3**	**1**	**5**	**2**
2	9+ **4**	**5**	**1**	**3**

111

+ − × ÷

2÷ **4**	**2**	60× **5**	2÷ **1**	3 **3**
4− **5**	**3**	**4**	**2**	7+ **1**
1	**5**	4− **3**	1− **4**	**2**
6× **3**	**1**	**2**	9+ **5**	**4**
2	4 **4**	9+ **1**	**3**	**5**

112

+ − × ÷

6+ 1	5	9+ 2	9+ 4	4+ 3
4 4	3+ 2	3	5	1
24× 2	1	4	4+ 3	3− 5
3	4	4− 5	1	2
2− 5	3	1	2÷ 2	4

115

+ − × ÷

16× 4	2	5 5	2− 3	1
2	12× 3	4	6+ 1	5
4− 5	1	2÷ 2	4	24× 3
60× 1	4	8+ 3	5	2
3	5	3+ 1	2	4

113

+ − × ÷

75× 5	3 3	3− 4	8+ 1	2
3	5	1	2	9+ 4
2÷ 4	2÷ 1	2	3	5
2	1− 4	3	9+ 5	1
3+ 1	2	9+ 5	4	3

116

+

14+ 5	11+ 3	4 4	3+ 1	2
2	4	3	9+ 5	6+ 1
3	3+ 2	1	4	5
4	1	10+ 5	9+ 2	3
6+ 1	5	2	3	4

114

+ − × ÷

75× 3	5	3+ 2	1	8× 4
5	1− 3	9+ 4	2	1
1 1	4	5	1− 3	2
2÷ 4	2÷ 2	1	9+ 5	8+ 3
2	2− 1	3	4	5

117

+

9+ 4	5	5+ 2	3	3+ 1
7+ 3	1	9+ 5	4	2
8+ 5	3	6+ 1	2	15+ 4
2	10+ 4	3	1	5
1	2	4	5	3 3

+

14+ 3	4	3+ 1	2	9+ 5
9+ 4	2	5	3	1
5	12+ 3	6+ 4	3+ 1	2
3+ 1	5	2	12+ 4	3
2	1	3	5	4 4

+ −

5+ 1	7+ 4	3	5 5	1− 2
4	3+ 2	13+ 5	1	3
1− 2	1	4	3	9+ 5
3	4− 5	1	2− 2	4
10+ 5	3	2	4	1 1

+

8+ 2	5+ 1	4	7+ 3	8+ 5
5	12+ 2	3+ 1	4	3
1	3	2	6+ 5	7+ 4
3	4	10+ 5	1	2
9+ 4	5	3	2	1

+ −

7+ 3	9+ 4	5	8+ 2	1
4	1− 2	3	2− 1	5
11+ 2	4− 5	1	3	4 4
5	3+ 1	2	1− 4	3
1	3	4 4	3− 5	2

+

8+ 5	3	9+ 4	6+ 1	2
8+ 4	2	5	3	8+ 1
2	6+ 5	1	4	3
11+ 1	4	3	7+ 2	5
3	3+ 1	2	9+ 5	4

+ −

3 2	5	1− 3	3− 1	4
7+ 5	1	2	1− 4	3
1	7+ 4	4− 5	1− 3	2 2
4 4	3	1	2	4− 5
1− 3	2	9+ 4	5	1

124

+ −

³3	⁹⁺5	4	³⁺1	2
⁴⁻5	1	¹¹⁺2	4	⁸⁺3
¹⁻2	3	⁴⁻1	5	4
²⁻4	2	5	¹³⁺3	1
³⁻1	4	3	2	5

125

+ −

⁷⁺4	³⁺2	1	⁴⁻5	⁵⁺3
3	¹⁻5	4	1	2
⁹⁺2	4	⁵5	²⁻3	1
⁴⁻1	3	⁸⁺2	4	¹⁻5
5	⁴⁺1	3	2	4

126

+ − × ÷

²÷2	¹⁻3	4	¹⁰ˣ5	1
4	¹⁰ˣ1	⁷⁺3	2	⁹⁺5
5	2	1	3	4
⁴⁻1	5	²÷2	4	⁶ˣ3
¹⁻3	4	⁵5	1	2

127

+ − × ÷

³⁰ˣ2	5	3	⁹⁺4	1
⁴⁻5	¹⁻3	²÷2	1	4
1	4	⁴⁻5	⁵⁺3	2
²⁴ˣ4	2	1	⁴⁰ˣ5	¹⁵ˣ3
3	1	4	2	5

128

+ − × ÷

²÷2	¹⁻4	²⁻3	⁴⁻1	5
4	5	1	⁶ˣ3	2
²⁻3	1	³⁻5	²÷2	³⁻4
⁸⁺5	3	2	4	1
⁷⁺1	2	4	²⁻5	3

129

+ − × ÷

²÷4	2	⁵5	²⁻3	1
⁴⁺3	1	⁴⁰ˣ2	5	4
³⁺1	¹⁻3	4	⁴⁰ˣ2	5
2	²⁰ˣ5	1	4	¹⁻3
⁵5	4	⁴⁺3	1	2

130

+ − × ÷

120× **3**	**4**	4− **1**	**5**	2÷ **2**
2	**5**	1− **4**	**3**	**1**
4− **5**	**1**	2÷ **2**	**4**	12+ **3**
8× **1**	2− **3**	**5**	2 **2**	**4**
4	**2**	4+ **3**	**1**	**5**

133

+ − × ÷

12× **4**	**3**	9+ **5**	2÷ **1**	**2**
2− **3**	**5**	**4**	2 **2**	6+ **1**
2÷ **2**	5+ **1**	1− **3**	1− **4**	**5**
1	**4**	**2**	**5**	1− **3**
3− **5**	**2**	2− **1**	**3**	**4**

131

+ − × ÷

10× **1**	**2**	60× **5**	**4**	**3**
9+ **4**	**5**	2÷ **1**	1− **3**	**2**
5	10+ **3**	**2**	50× **1**	3− **4**
1− **2**	**4**	**3**	**5**	**1**
3	5+ **1**	**4**	**2**	**5**

134

+ − × ÷

1− **4**	**5**	15× **3**	2÷ **1**	**2**
8+ **3**	7+ **2**	**1**	**5**	3− **4**
5	**3**	**2**	9+ **4**	**1**
2÷ **1**	1− **4**	**5**	**2**	8+ **3**
2	5+ **1**	**4**	**3**	**5**

132

+ − × ÷

15× **5**	**3**	3+ **1**	**2**	1− **4**
7+ **4**	**2**	6+ **5**	**1**	**3**
1	2− **5**	**3**	2÷ **4**	**2**
1− **3**	**4**	2÷ **2**	75× **5**	**1**
2÷ **2**	**1**	**4**	**3**	**5**

135

+ − × ÷

12× **3**	2− **5**	3+ **2**	**1**	40× **4**
4	**3**	5+ **1**	2− **5**	**2**
3+ **2**	1 **1**	**4**	**3**	**5**
1	1− **4**	**5**	2÷ **2**	2− **3**
5 **5**	1− **2**	**3**	**4**	**1**

136

+

11+ 5	6	5+ 2	3	5+ 1	4
7+ 3	5+ 1	4	8+ 2	6	5 5
4	13+ 5	4+ 3	1	6+ 2	7+ 6
3+ 2	3	5	11+ 6	4	1
1	10+ 4	6	5	5+ 3	2
6 6	3+ 2	1	12+ 4	5	3

139

+ −

5− 1	6	9+ 3	16+ 2	5	4
9+ 3	3− 4	6	3+ 1	2	5
6	1	1− 4	5	5+ 3	2
9+ 4	5	5+ 2	3	5− 1	6
5+ 2	3	5	6+ 6	16+ 4	4+ 1
7+ 5	2	1	4 4	6	3

137

+

8+ 5	3+ 1	11+ 3	6	2	5+ 4
3	2	9+ 5	4	11+ 6	1
7+ 4	3	3+ 1	2	5	8+ 6
7+ 1	11+ 5	6	7+ 3	4	2
6	10+ 4	2	6+ 5	1	8+ 3
8+ 2	6	4	4+ 1	3	5

140

+ − × ÷

72× 6	3	4	3+ 1	2	8+ 5
1− 2	5− 1	6	20× 4	5	3
3	120× 4	5	5− 6	1	2÷ 2
1− 5	6	3+ 1	2	3 3	4
4	7+ 5	2	2− 3	10+ 6	5− 1
2÷ 1	2	3 3	5	4	6

138

+ −

2− 6	4	12+ 5	2 2	4+ 3	1
2 2	3	4	5− 6	1	11+ 5
4+ 1	7+ 2	7+ 3	4	5 5	6
3	5	6 6	3+ 1	2	2− 4
1− 5	5− 6	1	8+ 3	10+ 4	2
4	3+ 1	2	5	6	3 3

141

+ − × ÷

6× 3	3− 5	2	5− 1	6	2÷ 4
1	2÷ 3	6	1− 5	4	2
2	3+ 1	1− 3	4	15× 5	5− 6
1− 4	2	5 5	3÷ 6	3	1
5	16+ 6	5+ 4	2	15× 1	3
6	4	1	5+ 3	2	5

142

`+ − × ÷`

5− 6	**10+** 1	4	**10+** 5	**6×** 3	2
1	**3** 3	5	2	**9+** 4	**120×** 6
2÷ 2	**4−** 6	**3÷** 1	3	5	4
4	2	3	**5−** 6	1	5
20× 5	4	**3+** 2	1	**2÷** 6	3
8+ 3	5	**24×** 6	4	**2÷** 2	1

145

`+ − × ÷`

16× 2	**2÷** 6	3	4	**1−** 5	**5−** 1
4	2	**15×** 5	1	3	6
6+ 1	**20×** 5	**2−** 4	6	**3+** 2	**6×** 3
5	4	**4−** 6	**2−** 3	1	2
3÷ 3	1	2	5	**24×** 6	4
3− 6	3	**3+** 1	2	**9+** 4	5

143

`+ − × ÷`

24× 4	6	**3÷** 2	**7+** 3	**50×** 5	1
3 3	**20×** 1	6	4	2	5
3÷ 2	4	1	**11+** 5	6	**9+** 3
6	5	**15×** 3	1	**72×** 4	2
3+ 1	2	5	6	3	4
2− 5	3	**2÷** 4	2	**5−** 1	6

146

`+ − × ÷`

2− 5	3	**2** 2	**11+** 6	**6×** 1	**2÷** 4
5− 6	**6+** 1	**14+** 4	5	3	2
1	5	6	4	2	**2−** 3
2− 2	**3−** 4	1	**2÷** 3	6	5
4	**10+** 2	3	**7+** 1	**11+** 5	6
3− 3	6	5	2	4	**1** 1

144

`+ − × ÷`

10× 2	**3÷** 1	3	**6** 6	**9+** 4	5
5	**1−** 3	**2÷** 2	4	**5−** 1	**2÷** 6
3÷ 1	2	**9+** 4	5	6	3
3	**24×** 4	**3÷** 6	2	**6+** 5	1
10+ 4	6	**6+** 5	1	**3** 3	**8+** 2
6	**5** 5	**3÷** 1	3	2	4

147

`+ − × ÷`

10× 5	2	**15+** 3	4	**5−** 1	6
5− 6	**6+** 1	2	**9+** 5	4	**1−** 3
1	5	6	**5+** 3	2	4
3 3	**24×** 6	**1−** 4	**5−** 1	**10+** 5	2
2÷ 2	4	5	6	3	**6+** 1
4	**3** 3	**9+** 1	2	6	5

148

+ − × ÷

2− 4	2	3 3	30× 5	1	6
3÷ 3	1	11+ 5	6	14+ 4	5+ 2
18× 1	10× 5	2	4	6	3
6	3	5+ 1	3+ 2	300× 5	4
4− 2	6	4	1	3	5
1− 5	4	2÷ 6	3	2÷ 2	1

149

+ − × ÷

5− 1	6	12× 4	11+ 5	3÷ 3	2− 2
10× 5	2	3	6	1	4
2− 3	5	2÷ 1	2	10+ 4	6
2÷ 2	1	3÷ 6	60× 4	5	3
2− 4	7+ 3	2	7+ 1	6	6+ 5
6	4	30× 5	3	2	1

150

+ − × ÷

3÷ 2	11+ 5	6	2÷ 4	3÷ 1	3
6	5+ 1	4	2	2− 3	5
3− 1	4	15× 3	5− 6	40× 5	3÷ 2
1− 4	2÷ 3	5	1	2	6
5	6	1− 2	3	4	3− 1
6× 3	2	1	1− 5	6	4

Printed in the United States
By Bookmasters